# LENTEN GUIDE FOR PARISH LEADERS

# Lenten Guide
# for Parish Leaders

*To Enrich the Liturgy of the Word*

## John Craghan

TWENTY-THIRD PUBLICATIONS
**Mystic, Connecticut**

Twenty-Third Publications
185 Willow Street
P.O. Box 180
Mystic, CT 06355
(203) 536-2611

ISBN 0-89622-455-4
Library of Congress Catalog Card Number 90-71399

# CONTENTS

# III

## PARISH PRAYER SERVICES IN LENT   29

# IV

## RESOURCES FOR SMALL GROUP LEADERS   37

# INTRODUCTION

As a pastoral leader in your parish you demonstrate both generosity and responsibility. Your generosity is evident in the time and care you take to make the lenten season a truly significant faith experience for the people. Your responsibility is clear in the way you respond to the felt needs of your community. To assume the task of preparing the lenten liturgy and helping your parishioners grow through the Scriptures is to take on the ministry of helping both individuals and the community to respond more fully and actively to the word of God.

As a pastoral leader you are a catalyst of grace. By your efforts you embark upon making the community more aware of its Christian dignity, and hence of its obligation to repent. By your energy you will help many people come to see the lenten season as a unique opportunity to react to God's call.

As a pastoral leader you are also the beneficiary of God's grace. In seeking to make the liturgy meaningful for others, you also commit yourself to hearing God's call. The God who addresses the community also addresses you. Hence you, too, are challenged to die and rise with the Lord.

---

1

This *Lenten Guide for Parish Leaders* is intended to help you prepare to lead your parish into this lenten journey. It is addressed to pastors and associate pastors, to parish liturgy committees, to DREs and catechists, to liturgical ministers, and to the leaders of small groups. It seeks to provide hints and suggestions for developing the rich contents of the lenten Sunday Scriptures.

This guide is, of course, not a final and definitive list of recommendations for the season of Lent. There are many areas of parish spiritual and liturgical life that it does not cover. It is not designed, for example, to replace or substitute for the celebration and documents of the RCIA. As an aid it has three goals—to enrich the Sunday Liturgy of the Word, to enhance the process of faith and Scripture sharing in small groups, and to help you root your own lenten ministry in the word of God. Flexibility is a needed quality in making use of this guide. You should feel free to make changes and thereby reflect your own particular parish assemblies.

Lent is a very special time in the church's life. It is our hope that this book will deepen your parish's involvement in the season and help you prepare to move on into the holy Triduum and the joy of the fifty days of Easter.

# I

# Liturgical Resources

**Introduction**
These resources are suggestions for the Sundays of Lent in year B. They cover three areas:

*Introduction to the Readings*
The introductions to the readings given here are short summaries of some of the important elements in the readings. They are offered as centering points for those who are preparing for liturgy. When offered to the assembly they might work best as items in the bulletin (for the current week or the week to come), rather than as mini-homilies during the liturgy itself.

*Penitential Rite*
Because Lent is essentially a time to prepare for renewing our baptismal commitment and because Lent is the time for the catechumen's final preparation for entrance into the church, the sprinkling ritual, particularly the second form, is appropriate for all the Sundays of Lent. However, in the event that the liturgical team decides in favor of this rite rather than the sprinkling, we will suggest penitential rites for the first five Sundays of Lent.

*General Intercessions*

These general intercessions are samples based on the liturgical readings. You must feel free to adapt these to the needs of your local community and the events of our world. The assembly should sense our call to pray for the worldwide church, the diocese, the local parish community, and the needs of people everywhere. In the general intercessions that follow, the prayers assigned to the "Leader" are most properly proclaimed by a deacon, cantor, or other person, such as a lector.

A caution is in order in all these areas: the liturgy should be allowed to speak for itself. Many of us have a tendency to verbalize, to speak too much, to explain rather than to allow mystery and symbol to speak. When used lavishly and well, our liturgical symbols and actions can speak with far greater power than can our words.

As always, the liturgical team should begin preparing with the church's liturgical documents, especially *The General Instruction of the Roman Missal*, the Introduction to the *Lectionary for Mass* (revised edition), the *Rite of Christian Initiation of Adults* (including the National Statutes for the Catechumenate in the United States), *Directory for Masses with Children, General Norms for the Liturgical Year, Music in Catholic Worship, Liturgical Music Today*, and *Environment and Art in Catholic Worship*. A thorough grounding in these documents will enrich parish liturgy immeasurably and help you make the most of this book as well.

# First Sunday of Lent

## Introduction to the Readings

In the first reading (Genesis 9:8–15) we hear of God's new relationship with humankind and the world of nature after the flood. We are challenged to accept God's grace and so turn our lives around.

In the second reading (1 Peter 3:18–22) we listen to God's action in Jesus as the basis for change. We are asked to model Jesus in his passion, death, resurrection, and exaltation.

In the gospel (Mark 1:12–15) we learn of Jesus' temptation in the desert and his proclamation of the kingdom. We are bidden to expect temptation and adopt a new way of thinking and acting grounded in the person of Jesus.

## Penitential Rite

Presider   To prepare ourselves for worship, let us call to mind our sins. (*Pause for silent reflection.*) For the times we refused to change our way of life and disregarded your gift of grace, we pray, Lord, have mercy.

All   Lord, have mercy.

Presider   For the times we refused to effect change in the lives of others and thus offer them hope, we pray, Christ, have mercy.

All   Christ, have mercy.

Presider   For the times we refused to base our need to change on the life and death of Jesus, we pray, Lord, have mercy.

All   Lord, have mercy.

Presider   May almighty God have mercy on us, forgive us our sins, and lead us to everlasting life.

All   Amen.


## General Intercessions

Presider   Lord, as we begin this first full week of Lent, we turn to you with our petitions and we pray, Lord, save us.

Leader   For the church throughout the world: that it may be an effective instrument for change in the lives of all people, we pray to the Lord.

All   Lord, save us.

Leader   For this diocese and all its parishes: that this Lent we may generously respond to the call to "Repent, and believe in the gospel," we pray to the Lord.

All   Lord, save us.

Leader   For this parish community: that this Lent we may become more caring agents of change in the lives of our sisters and brothers, we pray to the Lord.

All   Lord, save us.

Leader   For all who despair of change because of addictions:

that this Lent we may provide hope by seeing to their needs, we pray to the Lord.

**All**      Lord, save us.

*(Other petitions may be added as desired.)*

**Presider**      Gracious and loving God, we bring these petitions before you with the utmost confidence. We know that, having given us your Son, you will not deny what we ask for in his name. May your Son be our inspiration and guide in our effort to change. We ask this through Christ our Lord.

**All**      Amen.

## SECOND SUNDAY OF LENT

### Introduction to the Readings

The first reading (Genesis 22:1–2, 9a, 10–13, 15–18) recounts the story of Abraham's near sacrifice of Isaac. We are challenged to balance our relationships with God, family, and spouse.

The second reading (Romans 8:31–34) tells of God's actual sacrifice of the beloved Son. We are asked to believe that, because of that act, God will continue to provide for us.

The gospel (Mark 9:2–10) proclaims Jesus' unique bond with the Father in the scene of the Transfiguration. We are bidden to see that our relationship with God hinges on both suffering and glory.

### Penitential Rite

**Presider**      To prepare ourselves for worship, let us call to mind our sins. *(Pause for silent reflection.)* For the times we refused to balance our relationships and excluded you from our world of interest and concern, we pray, Lord, have mercy.

**All**      Lord, have mercy.

**Presider**      For the times we refused to balance our relationships and excluded our sisters and brothers from our world of interest and concern, we pray, Christ, have mercy.

All      Christ, have mercy.

Presider     For the times we refused to balance our relationships and excluded the natural world from our world of interest and concern, we pray, Lord, have mercy.

All      Lord, have mercy.

Presider     May almighty God have mercy on us, forgive us our sins, and lead us to everlasting life.

All      Amen.

## General Intercessions

Presider     Having heard your Word, Lord God, we turn to you with our petitions and we pray, Lord, save us.

Leader     For the church throughout the world: that it may attain a healthy relationship by seeing to the needs of both believers and unbelievers, we pray to the Lord.

All      Lord, save us.

Leader     For all national and international leaders: that they may balance their relationships with their communities by securing peace and justice, we pray to the Lord.

All      Lord, save us.

Leader     For this parish community: that we may see that our relationship with God is bound up with our relationships with one another, we pray to the Lord.

All      Lord, save us.

Leader     For all those filled with hatred and bitterness: that they may use this Lent to be reconciled with sisters and brothers and hence with God, we pray to the Lord.

All      Lord, save us.

*(Other petitions may be added as desired.)*

Presider     Generous and caring God, you offer us the model for balancing relationships in the love of the Trinity. We ask that your triune love may empower us to strike a balance in our relationships with all of humanity and the natural world. We ask this through Christ our Lord.

All       Amen.

# THIRD SUNDAY OF LENT

## Introduction to the Readings

The first reading (Exodus 20:1–17) is the giving of the Ten Commandments on Mount Sinai. We are challenged to see legislation in terms of a God who has acted on our behalf and for our common good.

The second reading (1 Corinthians 1:22–25) is Paul's rejection of the gospel in terms of popular philosophy. It is his insistence on the Good News in the setting of the cross. We are bidden to see the cross as the ultimate expression of doing God's will.

The gospel (John 2:13–25) is the account of Jesus' cleansing of the temple. We are urged to see the implications of doing God's will. In other words, Jesus' cleansing of the temple, an act of doing God's will, becomes the catalyst leading to his death.

## Penitential Rite

Presider   In order to praise and honor our God in this liturgy, let us first call to mind our sins. (*Pause for silent reflection.*) For the times we refused to do your will by focusing solely on our pleasures and desires, we pray, Lord, have mercy.

All        Lord, have mercy.

Presider   For the times we refused to do your will by not providing for the needs of our sisters and brothers, we pray, Christ, have mercy.

| | |
|---|---|
| All | Christ, have mercy. |
| Presider | For the times we refused to do your will by not searching for your presence in your laws and all genuine human laws, we pray, Lord, have mercy. |
| All | Lord, have mercy. |
| Presider | May almighty God have mercy on us, forgive us our sins, and lead us to everlasting life. |
| All | Amen. |

## General Intercessions

| | |
|---|---|
| Presider | Lord, aware of our continuous need of grace in doing your will, we make the following petitions and we pray, Lord, save us. |
| Leader | For the church throughout the world: that it may do your will by providing for the poor, sick, and mistreated of the globe, we pray to the Lord. |
| All | Lord, save us. |
| Leader | For all civil and ecclesiastical lawmakers: that they may do your will by incorporating true values in their legislation, we pray to the Lord. |
| All | Lord, save us. |
| Leader | For this parish community: that it may do your will by being a source of hope and encouragement to all hurting sisters and brothers, we pray to the Lord. |
| All | Lord, save us. |
| Leader | For all who have no regard for law: that they may see that to do your will is to ensure the good of the entire community, we pray to the Lord. |
| All | Lord, save us. |
| | *(Other petitions may be added as desired.)* |
| Presider | Gracious and loving God, you gently teach us that to do your will is to recognize your presence. We are especially reminded of what your Son said: "I came down from heaven...to do the will of the one who |

sent me." Help us to base our accomplishment of your will on the example of your Son. We ask this through Christ our Lord.

All        Amen.

## FOURTH SUNDAY OF LENT

### Introduction to the Readings

In the first reading (2 Chronicles 36:14–17, 19–23) we learn that the once distraught exiles are now empowered to return home and rebuild their temple. We are encouraged to believe our God is also a God of new beginnings.

In the second reading (Ephesians 2:4–10) we hear that God's enemies were brought to new life in the act of raising Jesus. We are called upon to believe that this same God continues to transform us with new life in the company of God's Son.

In the gospel (John 3:14–21) we are told that Jesus' passion and death are the start of his return to the Father and result in eternal life for the believer. We are challenged to believe that apparent tragedy can be the setting for new life.

### Penitential Rite

Presider    In order to enter into our God's presence in this act of worship, let us first call to mind our sins. *(Pause for silent reflection.)* For the times we refused to believe that you could turn evil into good, we pray, Lord, have mercy.

All        Lord, have mercy.

Presider    For the times we refused to acknowledge your presence in the midst of our wretchedness and despair, we pray, Christ, have mercy.

All        Christ, have mercy.

Presider    For the times we refused to trust that by your help our Good Fridays could become Easter Sundays, we pray, Lord, have mercy.

All        Lord, have mercy.

Presider    May almighty God have mercy on us, forgive us our sins, and lead us to everlasting life.

All        Amen.

## General Intercessions

Presider    Realizing your continual interest and concern in the events of our lives, we confidently make these petitions as we pray, Lord, hear our prayer.

Leader    For the church throughout the world: that it may be God's instrument for turning frustration and despair into trust and hope, we pray to the Lord.

All        Lord, hear our prayer.

Leader    For all world leaders: that by their practice of justice and compassion they may overcome the ravages of poverty and neglect, we pray to the Lord.

All        Lord, hear our prayer.

Leader    For this parish community: that it may be the agent of new life by attending to the needs of the distraught and the afflicted, we pray to the Lord.

All        Lord, hear our prayer.

Leader    For those who despair of the possibility of new beginnings: that they may come to believe that the cross moves on to the empty tomb, we pray to the Lord

All        Lord, hear our prayer.

*(Other petitions may be added as desired.)*

Presider    Merciful and compassionate God, you have the capacity to turn evil into good. Enable us to direct our lives by constantly clinging to that belief. Help us to see that Good Friday leads inexorably to Easter Sunday. We ask this through Christ our Lord.

All        Amen.

## FIFTH SUNDAY OF LENT

**Introduction to the Readings**

In the first reading (Jeremiah 31:31–34) we hear that the God of Israel, despite the sinfulness of the people, will renew the covenant and start over. We are called upon to believe this giver of gifts will do the same for us.

In the second reading (Hebrews 5:7–9) we learn that Jesus' humanity is truly a gift—he learned from the things he suffered. We are challenged to believe that our own weakness can be the manifestation of God's gift-giving.

In the gospel (John 12:20–33) we are told that Jesus' death will mean life for everyone and that the disciple must accept death to gain that life. We are bidden to see and acknowledge that our God can transform death into life.

**Penitential Rite**

Presider    To come into the presence of our God through this act of worship, let us call to mind our sins. *(Pause for silent reflection.)* For the times we refused to believe that you are truly a God of surprises, we pray, Lord, have mercy.

All         Lord, have mercy.

Presider    For the times we refused to dismiss our autonomy and control to focus on you as the giver of gifts, we pray, Christ, have mercy.

All         Christ, have mercy.

Presider    For the times we refused to acknowledge the gift of your Son by limiting ourselves merely to our efforts, not your grace, we pray, Lord, have mercy.

All         Lord, have mercy.

Presider    May almighty God have mercy on us, forgive us our sins, and lead us to everlasting life.

All         Amen.

**General Intercessions**

Presider    Lord, realizing that you are the great giver of gifts, we make the following petitions as we pray, Lord, hear our prayer.

Leader　For the church throughout the world: that it may emulate the giver of gifts by openness and expectation, not control, we pray to the Lord.

All　Lord, hear our prayer.

Leader　For all civil authorities: that they may follow the example of the giver of gifts by offering new hope to their people, not by oppressing them, we pray to the Lord.

All　Lord, hear our prayer.

Leader　For this parish community: that it may be receptive to the gifts of other parishioners and acknowledge them as gifts from our God, we pray to the Lord.

All　Lord, hear our prayer.

Leader　For all those obsessed with autonomy and independence: that they may find in believers people who lavish their gifts because of the giver of gifts, we pray to the Lord.

All　Lord, hear our prayer.

*(Other petitions may be added as desired.)*

Presider　Generous and loving God, we acknowledge you to be the giver of gifts. We realize this because you did not spare your Son but handed him over to death. In your kindness enable us to imitate the gift of his self-giving. We ask this through Christ our Lord.

All　Amen.

## Passion Sunday (palm sunday)

### Introduction to the Readings
In the first reading (Isaiah 50:4–7) we hear the account of the Suffering Servant who endures humiliations on behalf of the community. We are urged to make a great discovery by seeing his pain and tribulation as the manifestation of God's concern.

In the second reading (Philippians 2:6–11) we learn of Jesus as one who was glorified because he first emptied himself. We are challenged to see through the humiliation and make the great discovery of our God's presence.

In the gospel (Mark 14:1–15:47) we listen to the passion account according to Mark. We are called upon to see beyond the degradation and the abuse to confess with the centurion: "Truly this man was the Son of God!"

*(The Penitential Rite is omitted today in favor of the procession and blessing of branches or the solemn entrance.)*

## General Intercessions

| | |
|---|---|
| Presider | Lord, having heard the account of your Son's passion and death, we confidently bring these petitions before you as we pray, Lord, hear our prayer. |
| Leader | For the church throughout the world: that in times of persecution and oppression it may discover and manifest the presence of our God, we pray to the Lord. |
| All | Lord, hear our prayer. |
| Leader | For all civil authorities: that they may discover in the persons of the poor and the downtrodden the person of our God and that they may be moved to help, we pray to the Lord. |
| All | Lord, hear our prayer. |
| Leader | For this parish community: that it may discover, in the despairing and the anguishing people in its midst, a God who calls for the great discovery and thus a sense of involvement, we pray to the Lord. |
| All | Lord, hear our prayer. |
| Leader | For all those who experience the absence of God: that through our care and concern they may discover the presence of a concerned and committed God, we pray to the Lord. |
| All | Lord, hear our prayer. |

*(Other petitions may be added as desired.)*

Presider  Generous and loving God, you lead us to make the great discovery in the emptiness of the tomb on Easter morning. Support and enable us to make similar discoveries in the lives of our desperate sisters and brothers. We ask this through Christ our Lord.

All  Amen.

## II

# HOMILY SUGGESTIONS
# AND BACKGROUND NOTES
# ON THE READINGS

*These are not homilies intended to be given as they stand. A homily needs to address the concerns of a particular group of people in a given location, and only you can provide that personal dimension. These suggestions are given here to help you root yourself firmly in the Word of God so that you can be prepared to bring the message of the gospel to the lives of your people. As such, these suggestions should be of use, not only to those formally addressing the community at liturgy, but also to those preparing liturgy, and the leaders of faith and Scripture sharing groups as well.*

## FIRST SUNDAY OF LENT

Today's three readings deal with the reality of change. In the first reading God begins anew with humanity in the aftermath of the flood. The new covenantal relationship implies that people must live in accordance with the will of God. In the second reading the author encourages his audience to lead a life grounded in Jesus' exaltation at the Father's right hand. As baptized Christians, they must indeed transform their lives—their baptism is linked to that new creation begun by the resurrection of Jesus. There is the element of change in the gospel as well. Satan tries to swerve Jesus from following the will of his Father. In the proclamation of the kingdom, Jesus urges his audience to repent, to adopt a new way of thinking that impacts our way of acting.

It may be useful to touch upon our resistance to change. We humans tend to think that things are running smoothly and, hence, there is no need to change. Lent by its very nature presupposes the opposite. It is that unique time in the Christian calendar when we take time out to reassess our standing with God and the community. It is that special opportunity to examine those areas of our lives where our resistance to change is greatest.

What brings about change? Here we are probably prone to think about our own efforts. While this cannot be denied, our readings underline the other principle of change—God's grace. In the first reading God's covenant with humanity is not dictated by humans. It is God's free gift. In the second reading the ability to lead Christian lives is grounded in the death-resurrection-exaltation experience of Christ—Jesus leads sinners to God. In the gospel the capacity to repent is rooted in the gospel that becomes incarnate in Christ. While we must not disparage our own efforts, we must look to God's radical ability to transform us.

It is helpful to connect the theme of change with the celebration of eucharist. In faith we believe that the bread and the wine are changed into the body and blood of Christ. This change must, in turn, impact our need to change. Far from being abstract, this change in our lives rests upon the One who suffered and died and rose for us. To celebrate eucharist, therefore, is to celebrate this momentous change in the life of Jesus. The God who nourishes us is the God who provides the food and the drink for our change.

## SECOND SUNDAY OF LENT

In one way or another today's three readings have to do with the reality of balancing relationships. In the first reading Abraham must balance his relationships with his God, with his son Isaac, and (implicitly at least) with his wife Sarah. It is a delicate matter, since the sacrifice of Isaac would seem to destroy Abraham's relationship with his son and his wife. In the second reading Paul breaks out into a hymn about God's all-powerful love, a love that balances relationships. To have a relationship with God is to be able to overcome any and all opposition.

After all, this time, God (unlike in the story of Abraham) does not spare the Son. In the gospel the Father solemnly proclaims that Jesus is indeed his beloved Son. However, the relationship between the Father and Jesus hinges on Jesus' forthcoming passion and death. The reality of the cross is also the believer's bond with Jesus and hence the believer's relationship with Jesus.

Think about our human perception of relationships. It seems to be our common experience that things go well for us whenever we balance our relationships. Thus, when our relationships with spouse, family, friends, and community are properly aligned, we truly enjoy life. Perhaps our temptation is to attempt to have a one-on-one relationship with our God and to neglect our other human relationships. However, the reality of the Christian life is that the only way to be related properly to this God is to be related properly to this God's family, and that means everyone.

What are the obstacles to balancing our relationships? A few of them include unwillingness to communicate and dialogue, focus on self to the neglect of others, blindness to the real needs of others, lack of awareness of our God's presence and of that presence in others. Lent is a very special time to reflect on those relationships where these and similar obstacles keep us from being fully human and fully Christian.

Eucharist, by its very nature, deals with relationships. The believer clearly has a relationship with the entire Trinity. However, the believer at eucharist cannot worship in isolation. The believer necessarily rubs elbows with the entire community. To participate fully in eucharist is to renew our efforts at balancing our relationships with the community. After all, we come together on Sunday as sisters and brothers. Eucharist powerfully reminds us that blood is thicker than water.

## THIRD SUNDAY OF LENT

One common thread uniting all three readings is the doing of God's will. In the first reading there is the proclamation of the Ten Commandments on Mount Sinai. The covenant bond between Yahweh and Israel depends on doing the will of this God who acted on their behalf through the Exodus. In the second reading there is Paul's insistence on the centrality of the crucified Jesus. To preach such a Jesus, and thus do God's will, occasions obstacles for the Jews and appears totally irrational to the Greeks. In the gospel there is Jesus' cleansing of the temple. For Jesus, doing God's will means undertaking such an action, for the people are making his Father's house a marketplace. Carrying out his Father's will, however, also implies Jesus' forthcoming passion and death—the time when Jesus will be consumed.

The homilist may elect to focus on our human resistance to doing God's will. Our society exalts the values of autonomy and freedom. As a result, we want to be in complete charge and have total control. We want to determine our own destiny as far as possible. Historically, however, unbridled autonomy usually leads to disaster. As for the matter of freedom, we generally think of freedom in terms of being free *from*. For example, on vacation, we are free from our regular work. Having paid our taxes, we are free from the IRS. The perfection of freedom, however, resides in being free *for*. This means, in part, being free for our family and community, being free for those who are in need. Basically, to do God's will is to exercise this freedom for our God and others.

Doing God's will often conjures up the reality of laws. Besides viewing them as impediments to our drive for autonomy, we also seem to see them as impersonal. We keep the law—and hence do God's will—because we know the consequences of non-compliance. Here our challenge is to examine the values behind laws. For example, do we attend Mass on Sunday because church law commands us or do we celebrate the eucharist because we feel the need to be nourished by a loving God? Do we observe the speed laws because we want to avoid a ticket or do we keep them because we want to assure the safety of others? Ultimately we must see all just laws as being grounded in our God. If God prefaces the Ten Commandments with: "I, the Lord, am your God, who brought you out of the land of Egypt," should we not preface all genuine laws with: "I am Jesus, your brother, who suffered, died, and rose for you"?

Eucharist has much to do with God's will. We simply link the Upper Room with the agony in the garden. Jesus is one who teaches genuine freedom: "This is my blood of the covenant, which will be shed for many" (Mark 14:24). Jesus is the one who exemplified the doing of his Father's will: "Abba, Father…Take this cup away from me, but not what I will but what you will" (Mark 14:36). To celebrate eucharist is to allow Jesus' experience to impact our entire way of life.

## FOURTH SUNDAY OF LENT

Among other themes, that of receiving new life is conspicuous. In the first reading the exiles are languishing in Babylon. However, with the ascendancy of the Persian king Cyrus, there is new life—some will soon depart for their homeland and participate in the rebuilding of the temple. In the second reading there is the vivid contrast between human weakness and God's all-powerful activity. At a time when the recipients of Paul's letter were God's enemies, he brought them to life together with Christ, raised them together with Christ, and enthroned them together with Christ. In the gospel there is the link between Jesus' death and new life for believers. Jesus' "being lifted up" initiates the return to the Father that, in turn, results in life for those who believe.

The homilist or leader may call to mind some events that initially appear to preclude new life. One can easily bring to mind the lingering illness of a loved one, the death of a spouse or child, the loss of a good position, the demise of friendship, etc. Given such experiences, we find it exceedingly difficult to believe that new life can emerge in the aftermath of death. Despair and helplessness are apparently in control.

Our own sinfulness may also be an obstacle to new life. We know from our past history how often we have fallen despite a multitude of good intentions. Our weakness becomes such a glaring reality that renewal, by definition, seems out of the question. In this situation God seems to be more and more distant from our "real" world.

Lent is that rich opportunity when we dare to believe, not in a God of endings, but in a God of new beginnings. Are we really that different from the exiles who imagined that the end had come? But God has raised us up together with Christ.

We are intimately involved in that action whereby Good Friday is swallowed up in the contagious joy of Easter Sunday. We are challenged to believe that Good Friday in our lives moves inexorably toward Easter Sunday. The empty tomb means bountiful new life.

Eucharist captures that movement from death to life. We hear the words of institution that interpret Jesus' self-giving in passion and death. But after "Christ has died" we immediately add "Christ is risen." Eucharist is intended to empower us in the face of our death experiences. Eucharist makes us capable of new life since we draw our life from him who was lifted up for us. Eucharist nourishes us to make us capable of finding life where only death previously held sway.

## FIFTH SUNDAY OF LENT

One theme that appears to spring from the three readings is that of handling gifts. In the face of our own efforts at control and autonomy we learn of a God who gives gifts because that is the nature of this God. In the first reading Jeremiah speaks of a "new covenant." Israel is so mired in sin that only God's unmerited action will make it possible to start a new relationship. In the second reading the gift is Jesus' humanity. The author of Hebrews reminds us that Jesus the high priest has so much solidarity with his sisters and brothers that he must offer prayers and supplications with loud cries and tears. This same author later assures us that Jesus can indeed sympathize with our weaknesses. In the gospel the gift comes in the form of Jesus' fear in the face of passion and death. Like us, he is tempted to depart from his Father's plan. He goes on to pray that he may carry out his Father's will. The gift is also in the Father's promise that he has glorified Jesus and that he will continue to do so. The gift is Jesus' death that allows him to draw everyone to himself.

The homilist may choose to point out why we seem to resist gift-giving. Often it is because of our exaggerated sense of autonomy. We do not want to be surprised. To be surprised means not to be in full control of the situation. To receive a gift is to admit quite candidly that someone else can influence our destiny and thus jeopardize our independence.

Our own weakness may preclude our capacity to handle gifts. For one reason or another we do not dare to imagine that we are worthy of love. After all, to give gifts freely is to manifest love. Here we might take up the weakness aspect of the second reading and gospel. The Jesus of Hebrews and John must contend with pain and fear. In this state he must look beyond his own efforts to a Father who gives since it is the nature of God to give. The Jesus of these writings is indeed one whom we can admire and imitate. Here the bond of solidarity is the bond of weakness.

In eucharist we are concerned with gifts and gift-giving. We speak of the eucharistic gifts and we proclaim the self-giving of Jesus—he is given up for us. Eucharist, therefore, allows us to accept God's gift and to perceive our autonomy and weakness in a new light. Eucharist also directs gift-giving in another direction. Because we celebrate eucharist in community and as community, we are challenged to give gifts to those who need them. To respond to the prayer of the faithful with "Lord, hear our prayer" is to commit ourselves to action on behalf of those who perhaps do not dare to think of gifts. To give gifts to such people is to imitate the giver of gifts. Perhaps we should add in some way to our creed: we believe in a God of surprises who empowers us to surprise others.

## PASSION SUNDAY (PALM SUNDAY)

One theme that emerges from our three readings is that of making discoveries. In the first reading we hear about Isaiah's Suffering Servant. He is the object of ridicule and abuse, and these suggest that God has abandoned him. But in the end we discover that God will exonerate him—after all, he bore, not his own guilt, but the guilt of the community. In the second reading Paul adapts an early Christian hymn to demonstrate a great discovery. Refusing the prerogatives of divine honor, Jesus empties himself, embraces death, indeed death on a cross. What follows is the great discovery. This Jesus receives the title of "Lord"— one previously reserved to God alone. In Mark's passion account there is the abandonment of Jesus in the garden. In the Jewish trial there is the recognition of Jesus as Messiah, Son of the Blessed One, and Son of Man—but it is a recognition that leads to charges of blasphemy. In the Roman trial Jesus receives the "royal" treatment with mantle, crown, and "homage" of the soldiers. But the great discovery is the centurion's confession: "Truly this man was the Son of God!"

It may be appropriate to direct attention to those situations where we do not expect to make discoveries because of our prejudice. We may bypass the poor—they upset us by not reaching the proper status. We may neglect the disillusioned—they revolt us by not keeping the proper balance. We may turn off society's rejects—they make us uneasy by not projecting the proper image. We are really not that different from the audience of the Suffering Servant and the audience of Jesus of Nazareth.

Lent, especially Holy Week, is an apt time for scrutinizing our prejudices. The basic issue seems to be: how will our God be manifested? We program and condition our God to be manifest only in the "nice" people. To that extent we are unwilling to make discoveries. Lent allows us to see the glory of the empty tomb in the pain of the wood of the cross. Lent is intended to energize us to see our God present in the less than beautiful people. Lent is calculated to empower us to discover our God in the hurting and downtrodden.

Eucharist deals with making discoveries. In faith, our discovery is that the bread and the wine are now the body and blood of Jesus. This is a discovery that enables us to pierce the externals and penetrate to the Risen One in our midst. Because we celebrate eucharist in community, we are bidden to look to our sisters and brothers. We are challenged to make the great discovery by seeing them as manifestations of our God, especially those who need our love and support. Eucharist is the sacrament wherein we must put aside our prejudices and presuppositions.

# EASTER SUNDAY

Today's three readings and responsorial psalm focus on the significance of change or transformation. In the first reading Luke provides a resumé of Jesus' ministry (Acts 10:37–39). However, he quickly adds that God transformed the killing of Jesus into resurrection, an event through which believers gain life. In the responsorial psalm (Psalm 118) the author sings of God's marvelous intervention on behalf of the king and the community—it is a change that is nothing short of miraculous. "The stone which the builders rejected has become the cornerstone" (v 22). In the second reading (1 Corinthians 5:6-8) Paul speaks of God's action in Jesus as a Passover sacrifice. He sees this feast as a trek that goes from death to life. It is that transformation that God through Christ holds out to believers. In the gospel (16:1–8) Mark paradoxically contrasts the Crucified One with the Risen One. For Mark the resurrection is not the final moment—believers must appropriate this transformation to their own way of life.

The homilist or leader may choose to emphasize the symbols of the renewal of baptismal vows and the sprinkling with the Easter water. The renewal of vows calls to mind our baptism when we resolved to live in the freedom of God's children—a freedom that necessarily involves change or transformation. The Easter water recalls the resurrection experience of Jesus and how we share in the event together with Jesus. As a result, we are bidden to reflect the change that has occurred in Jesus.

The homilist or leader may elect to direct attention to the lenten experience. Which areas in our lives called for the greatest change? Here it may be useful to focus on principal areas rather than a variety of lesser ones. The homilist may want to encourage the community to continue to work on those changes. To be sure, this will not be by dint of one's efforts only. It is the unique grace of the resurrection that makes transformation possible. We who have risen with Christ are capable of change in and through Christ.

The eucharist and transformation go hand in hand. The symbols of food and drink imply the nourishment needed to effect change. But they are nourishment rooted in the passion, death, and resurrection of Jesus. To share the bread and the wine is to participate in those events by which the Father sustains the Son and transforms death into new life. Eucharist is a communal enterprise. We interact with the members of the community and thereby can enjoy the support and help without which change is impossible. To that extent change never happens in isolation.

# Homily Suggestions and Background Notes for the Third, Fourth, and Fifth Sundays of Lent, Year A

*In parishes celebrating with the elect who are preparing for initiation at the Easter Vigil, the scrutinies are celebrated on the Third, Fourth, and Fifth Sundays of Lent. When the scrutinies are celebrated, the readings for Year A are used (RCIA #143, 146). Even when the scrutinies are not celebrated, the A readings may be used on these Sundays.*

## THIRD SUNDAY OF LENT (YEAR A)

All three readings focus on the symbols of water, thirst, and pouring. In the first reading, the Israelite community finds itself in need of water during the desert wandering. Mother Yahweh satisfies their needs by providing water from the rock. In the second reading, Paul speaks of the love of God that has been poured into our hearts through the Holy Spirit. Elsewhere (see 1 Corinthians 12:13) he speaks of drinking from the one Spirit. In the gospel, John narrates the story of the Samaritan woman. Jesus slakes her thirst—however, she moves from a crass material conception of water to a more spiritual one, that of Jesus as the source of living water. Eventually the woman satisfies the thirst of her community. She acts as an apostle by bringing them to Jesus.

Try to apply these symbols of water, thirst, and pouring to the needs of the community. We all have various types of thirst. We may need encouragement, consolation, and understanding. Through baptism we assume the obligation to live in community and thus address the problems of community. Like Mother Yahweh and Jesus, we are empowered to reach out and satisfy. The homilist may choose to point out some serious concerns in the local community that need attention. By alleviating the thirst of those in community, we are sharing the revelation that Jesus gave to the Samaritan woman.

Think about the past experiences of individuals or the community. Recall those instances when others saw our situation and acted on our behalf. Parents, family members, and friends may provide good examples of living out the baptismal commitment by slaking the thirst of others.

There is a clear link to the eucharist. In eucharist Jesus satisfies our hunger and our thirst. However, such satisfaction is the empowerment to go forth from eucharist and reenact Jesus' compassion in our family, community, etc. To have one's thirst slaked means to slake the thirst of others.

With an eye to the scrutinies of the RCIA, the homilist may want to emphasize the symbols of water and thirst. Like the woman of Samaria, the elect who are also thirsting for living water are challenged to turn to the Lord and hear his word. Ultimately, Jesus is the only fountain that can slake their thirst. After the manner of the Samaritan woman the elect are called to review their lives before Christ and acknowledge their sins. In the other direction, the elect must share with their friends and families the marvel of their own encounter with Christ. Thus the eternal water they receive from Christ will impact others. To that extent—like the Samaritan woman—they become apostles.

## FOURTH SUNDAY OF LENT (YEAR A)

All three readings deal with light or seeing. In the first reading, the prophet Samuel looks only at externals as he seeks to find a king to replace Saul. While humans concentrate on the exterior, the Lord looks into the heart. In the second reading, the author of Ephesians describes the radical conversion demanded of the baptized. They are to live as children of the light. They are also to expose evil by projecting their light. In the gospel, John tells the account of the man born blind. By acknowledging Jesus in a progressive manner, he steadily advances from darkness to light. For him Jesus is indeed the light of the world.

Perhaps the homilist could point to different experiences of darkness among the members of the community. One may think of local power failures or those blackouts that affect large cities. In such circumstances we place a higher priority on matches, candles, flashlights, small generators, and the like. We know how people emerge as heroes during such times of crisis. Darkness thus becomes a faith opportunity.

The homilist may want to refer to the second reading where the baptized are called the children of light. We are called upon to project the light of Christ by our lifestyle. To offer hope to the depressed, to visit the shut-ins, to console the sick and the dying are to illuminate our world with the light of Christ.

The homilist may choose to focus, in part, on the first reading. We all have the natural tendency to judge only on the basis of externals, and we know from experience that we have made mistakes in this process. What our faith demands, however, is that we assume new spectacles. With such spectacles we are to begin by asking, "What good points does this person have?" To judge others in this way is to appreciate the infinite variety of others' gifts.

During the forthcoming event of the Easter Vigil, we will celebrate the resurrection, in part, by speaking of Jesus as the new light. With our candles we will all share in that light. With those same candles we will renew our baptismal vows and welcome new life born of water and the spirit. On this most sacred night we repeat our obligation to light up the world of others.

Keeping in mind the scrutinies of the RCIA, the homilist may use to great advantage the symbols of light and seeing. Thus the elect are called upon to recognize Jesus as the source of light who dispels the darkness in their hearts. Like the man born blind, the elect are to acknowledge the Good News that is Jesus and share it with their world. This Good News consists in this: through the death and resurrection of Jesus the light of truth and love is accessible to humanity. It is through this light that they will ultimately see God face to face.

## FIFTH SUNDAY OF LENT (YEAR A)

All three readings focus on life, death, and resurrection. In the first reading, Ezekiel addresses a message of hope to his community. Although they describe themselves as dried up bones, God will raise up the exiles, breathe upon them, and eventually restore them to their land. In the second reading, Paul announces that Christians are right with God because of Christ's self-giving. Because of that gift they are to let the Spirit work its transforming effect. That Spirit who raised Jesus from the dead will also raise believers from the dead. In the gospel, John narrates the story of the raising of Lazarus. This raising is but a token of that genuine life that the risen Lord will eventually give to all who believe in him. To accept Jesus as the resurrection and the life is to share ultimately in the resurrection experience of Jesus.

The homilist may choose to describe the significance of the resurrection of the body. It is unlike the experience of Lazarus, because he will die again. To be raised is to be transformed. It is to enter into that process by which Jesus returns exalted to the Father. Resurrection is thereby a community happening. We do not go to heaven single file. We do not experience resurrection as isolated individuals. We share in Christ's glory because we belong to his body, the church.

It may be helpful to emphasize the hope of the resurrection for those who have lost family members or friends in death. The reality of the resurrection is that we continue to be a people of hope. Because of the empty tomb we can begin to look forward to reunion with our loved ones. This indeed offers the possibility of a full life.

The homilist or leader may want to use the metaphor of death and resurrection to describe those who exist but do not really live. All those who harbor hate, who refuse to speak to others, who feel cut off from community exist physically but they are not genuinely living. Resurrection for them can mean the offer of the gift of reconciliation to others and thus reinstatement into community.

It may be useful to refer to the acclamation after the consecration— "Christ has died, Christ is risen, Christ will come again." We are caught between the resurrection of Jesus and his second coming. In the meantime we are full of hope. Eucharist sustains us for living lives charged with hope as we anticipate the second coming. Eucharist also empowers us for sharing that hope now with sisters and brothers.

With a view to the scrutinies of the RCIA, the homilist may choose to link the life, death, and resurrection of Jesus to the needs of the elect. With the hope of the life-giving Spirit the elect are to prepare themselves for their birth to new life. Baptism, therefore, entails death to sin and life to God through Christ. In anticipating the eucharist, the elect will experience that unity with Christ who is the source of life and resurrection. In their lifestyle the elect are to manifest to the world the power of the risen Lord. It is this power that will enable them to cope with death and look forward to that unending life captured in the resurrection of the Lord.

# III

# Parish Prayer Services in Lent

## Preparing for Lent

*This brief prayer outline is intended for use by parish teams, liturgy commit-tees, small group leaders and others involved in planning and preparing for the parish's celebration of Lent.*

## Introduction

Leader    O God, our creator and redeemer, we acknowledge your presence in our midst. We fully realize that you seek to speak to us at all times, but in a very special way during the coming season of Lent. As we plan and prepare for our parish's celebration of this holy season, we ask your blessing on our work, which is also your work. We ask this through Christ our Lord.

All    Amen.

**Reading**

Reader     A reading from...(*Here it may be appropriate to select a biblical passage dealing with the call to repentance. The following may serve this end: Matthew 4:12–17; Mark 1:14–15; Luke 4:14–19.*)

(*After the reading it is helpful to provide for some silent time.*)

Leader     Having heard your Word, we turn to you with the greatest confidence and make the following petitions:

For the church throughout the world: that this Lent may be a time of genuine conversion for all Christians, we pray to the Lord.

All        Lord, hear our prayer.

Leader     For the faith community that we serve: that it may respond generously to the Lord's call to repentance during this season, we pray to the Lord.

All        Lord, hear our prayer.

Leader     For ourselves: that we may use our time and talent for both the good of the community and our own growth, we pray to the Lord.

All        Lord, hear our prayer.

(*Here the leader can invite participants to offer any petitions they wish. Some quiet time should be allowed for this to take place.*)

All        Lord, hear our prayer.

Leader     Lord, we praise and thank you for your concern about our deliberations. We take courage from knowing that our work is also your work. We know, therefore, that you will not cease to assist us in this our common venture. We pray this in the name of Jesus the Lord.

All        Amen.

## PRAYER AT THE END OF LENT

*This prayer outline is designed for use during or near the end of Lent. It is appropriate for small groups, for liturgy committees, for training and follow-up sessions with small group leaders, or for closing the lenten season with all the parish's small groups gathered together.*

### Introduction

Leader    Lent is God's gift to us. It is that special season in which we recall the culminating events in the life of Jesus. It is that grace-filled time when we remember the depth of God's love for us. It is that unique occasion when we advance from Calvary to the empty tomb, not only in the life of Jesus, but in our own lives as well.

Lent allows us to inventory our pluses and minuses. It permits us to look ever deeper into our relationship with God and our relationship with our sisters and brothers. Lent challenges us to correct our faults and develop new strategies for living out the plan of salvation.

Given this gift of Lent, we must break out into praise of our God. We must thank this God who through the church calls us to closer union with God and all of humanity. To praise is to acknowledge God's presence in our midst. To praise is to create an atmosphere in which we freely raise our voice in awe and amazement.

Aware of God's overwhelming goodness to us, we gratefully acknowledge our indebtedness.

Lector    For your gift of creation that is ongoing in your concern for us and especially in your forgiveness, we pray:

All    We praise you, Lord.

Lector    For the gift of your Son who constantly reminds us of your love for us, we pray:

All    We praise you, Lord.

Lector    For the gift of your Spirit, who ever brings to mind your changing of chaos into cosmos, we pray:

All        We praise you, Lord.

Lector        For the gift of our brothers and sisters who always make us aware of the multiplicity and variety of your gifts, we pray:

All        We praise you, Lord.

Leader        Gracious and loving God, enable us to appreciate more fully your gift of Lent. Allow us to respond more generously to your call for renewal and conversion. Grant us the grace to die once again with your Son to ourselves and to rise once again with your Son to love and service of all humanity. We ask this through Christ our Lord.

All        Amen.

## COMMUNAL PENANCE SERVICE

*The parish communal penance service might well be celebrated on Passion Sunday evening or on Monday, Tuesday, or Wednesday of Holy Week. Coming toward the end of the lenten experience but before the major days of Holy Week, this liturgy serves both as a response to the gospel's call to conversion and as a preparation for the great celebrations of the Triduum.*

*The ritual for the penance service is built around the readings. Those preparing this liturgy will be greatly assisted by* The Rites of the Catholic Church as Revised by the Second Vatican Ecumenical Council *(Pueblo Publishing, N.Y., 1976). The ritual contains some eighty pages of suggestions regarding the order, prayers, readings, examination of conscience, and other aspects of the penance service.*

### Introduction
*The entrance procession may be done either in silence or with an appropriate hymn. The presider greets the community, saying, for example:*

Presider     Grace, mercy, and peace be with you from God our Father and Our Lord Jesus Christ.

All     And also with you.

Presider     *(The opening prayer may be introduced with these or similar words:)* Sisters and brothers, our God has called us to conversion, to adopt a new way of thinking and acting. Let us beseech this God to grant us the grace of genuine conversion.

    *(Silent prayer follows, and then the opening prayer.)*

    Gracious and loving God, you have called us to a special relationship with you and with our sisters and brothers. We are painfully aware that our sins disrupt that bond not only with you but also with our sisters and brothers. Grant us your grace so that we may truly acknowledge our sinfulness and thus renew that special bond with you as well as with our sisters and brothers. We ask this through Christ our Lord.

All     Amen.

## Readings

*Two readings are recommended and a sung response following the first response is very appropriate. Appropriate readings dealing with conversion and renewal might include the following: Old Testament: Isaiah 40:1–11; Jeremiah 31:15–22; Hosea 14:2–9; New Testament: Luke 15:1–32 (the parables of the lost sheep, the lost coin, and the lost son); John 4:5–42 (the story of the Samaritan Woman).*

*The homily follows and is meant to help penitents experience God's great love for them and to enable them to open their hearts to receive God's gifts of sorrow for sin and conversion of life.*

## Examination of Conscience

*Silent time is very important here. However, it is also appropriate for the lector, deacon, or cantor to assist the penitents with a list of brief statements or a kind of litany. Here are some samples:*

Have I taken time to allow God to enter my life and to express my love for the Lord through daily prayer?

In walking my daily journey, have I tried to keep my relationship with God as first and most important?

Have I worshiped God with my sisters and brothers in the faith community on Sundays and days of obligation?

Have I prayed with my spouse and children?

Have I honored God by honoring the poor and those in need?

Have I tried to help my parents?

Have I honored God by respecting the good name of my neighbors, co-workers, classmates, and other persons in my life?

As a married person, have I honored God by respecting and loving my spouse and the commitment we have made to each other?

As a single person, have I respected the person and dignity of others as well as my own?

Have I allowed greed or sensuality to dominate my life?

Have I shared part of my time and talent with other needy persons in the community ?

*These or other similar brief statements can help the penitents examine their lives and ask more deeply for God's forgiveness.*

## General Confession of Sins

*The community is invited to kneel for a confession prayer such as the Confiteor (I confess to almighty God…) or the Act of Contrition (O my God, I am heartily sorry…).*

**Litany**

*Following the confessional prayer, the community is invited to stand for either a song or a litany. The litany may be both introduced and led by the cantor or lector. The following is an example:*

Leader    Our God loves us to such a degree that God gave us the Son. Let us implore this compassionate and reconciling God to forgive our sins and to let the Holy Spirit introduce genuine peace and love in our lives. Let us ask this God for the grace of true conversion.

All    We pray you, Lord, hear us.

Leader    Enable us to understand in an ever deeper way the truth that by our sins we offend not only God but also our sisters and brothers.

All    We pray you, Lord, hear us.

Leader    In being compassionate to us, help us to realize that, in turn, we must be compassionate to all.

All    We pray you, Lord, hear us.

Leader    In being reconciled with you, show us that we must also be reconciled with our sisters and brothers.

All    We pray you, Lord, hear us.

Leader    Let us now pray to God in the words Jesus gave us, asking for forgiveness and protection from all evil.

All    Our Father...

Presider    Gracious God, look kindly upon the sisters and brothers of your Son who implore you for forgiveness of their sins. Through the ministry of your church wipe away their faults and renew them with the presence of your Spirit. Empower us to move from acknowledgment of our sins to praise of you who never cease to love us. We ask this through Christ our Lord.

All:    Amen.

**Confession and Absolution**

*Individual confession and absolution now take place. The ritual calls for individual confession, but also the acceptance of a fitting act of satisfaction and ab-*

*solution with the priest extending his hands (or at least his right hand) over the penitent's head.*

### Proclamation of Praise

*Sing an appropriate canticle, hymn, or psalm of praise. Choose one that the people know well.*

## Concluding Prayer

Presider    By forgiving our sins, Lord God, you continue in a marvelous way the work of creation. We thank you for sending your Spirit upon us. We praise you for seeing in us the sisters and brothers of your Son. May we go forth in the love of this Trinity. We ask this through Christ our Lord.

All            Amen.

### Blessing and Dismissal

*The final blessing and dismissal follow very much as at the Sunday liturgy, and a recessional hymn may be used.*

# IV

# RESOURCES FOR SMALL GROUP LEADERS

### Introduction
Time, energy, and leadership are needed to build a strong parish program for Lent. And one of the best ways to help Lent come alive for parishioners is by fostering faith and Scripture sharing groups. Through RENEW and other programs, and most especially through the RCIA, we are relearning how very appropriate it is to celebrate Lent in a group, to reflect on and share stories about the significance of the gospel.

Parish councils, liturgy committee members, and small, faith-sharing groups of parishioners can all benefit from taking the lenten journey together. Your parish may already have such small Christian communities. If you are forming new groups, keep in mind that each group will need a designated leader, at least in the beginning. If you need leaders, putting a notice in the bulletin will help, but it is not an effective substitute for a personal invitation.

### Training
A training session is important, even for those who have led small groups in the past. Use this training session as an opportunity to thank

---

the leaders, to inspire them, and to help them review their duties as small group leaders. For those who cannot come to the scheduled meeting, another date should be found to assure that each small group leader is prepared.

The following material may be helpful both in the training process and in the actual small group meetings.

**1) Introductions at the First Meeting**     At the first meeting of your small group, it is good to take some time for introductions. The creation of a simple "Let's Get Acquainted" form will help you with this. The form should invite each person to write down (1) his or her name and the name by which he or she likes to be called; (2) one or two reasons why they chose to join a small group this Lent; and (3) one or two good things that have happened to them during the past month. Make enough forms for everyone in the group.

Distribute the "Let's Get Acquainted" cards and pencils, and let each person take a few minutes to fill it out.

The leader can begin the response to this by telling the group what he or she put down on the card. Then others can follow, in no particular order, until everyone has had a chance to speak.

**2) Ice-Breaking at Subsequent Meetings**     Things happen in people's lives and these things affect them. Perhaps one has had a death among relatives, or sickness at home; perhaps someone has received a promotion. All these things are important to the person and to the group. It is good to "take the temperature" of a group whenever that group assembles.

At the second meeting, the leader may simply ask, "How has your past week been? Is there one thing that stands out in your mind that has happened during this past week that you would like to mention?"

At this point, some silent time is in order. You have asked a question and it is good to let people think about it. It may be that someone else in the group will just break in and begin, but if not, then it may be better for the leader to go first. After the first few times, however, as a rule, the leader should not try to go first.

This "temperature taking" will take more or less time, depending on the group and their experiences of the past week. The leader need not worry that this is taking too much or too little time, or about getting through this section so that the group can get on to the formal discussion. Sharing is an important element of the small group, and this "temperature taking" can be a time for some significant sharing.

**3) Prayer Time**     Prayer helps to center us, and to get us in touch with God. Just as the Sunday liturgy invites us to have a gathering song and prayer before we hear the Word and the homily, so our meetings should offer the participants time for centering before they get into the evening's discussion.

The following is one example of a prayer outline that can be used after the introductions or ice-breaking experience. (Other sample prayer services for each of the weeks of Lent can be found starting on page 41.)

| | |
|---|---|
| All | Come, Holy Spirit, enkindle the fire of your love in the hearts of the faithful, and you shall renew the face of the earth. |
| Leader | Let us pray. O Lord, we ask you, send your Holy Spirit upon us, that we who are gathered in your name may be inspired by the Spirit's divine inspiration. We ask this through Christ our Lord. |
| All | Amen. |

Here is another example:

| | |
|---|---|
| Leader | Let us pray. O Lord, pour forth your Spirit upon us that we to whom the Incarnation of your Son was made known by the message of an angel may, by his passion and death, be brought to the glory of his resurrection. We ask this through Christ our Lord. |
| All | Amen. |
| Reader | A reading from... |
| | (*Here read the Scripture selections for the coming Sunday or at least the gospel and allow silent time after the reading.*) |
| Leader | Lord, God, we ask you to hear us now as we turn to you with our prayers and our petitions. |
| Reader | For the church throughout the world: that this Lent may be a time of conversion and growth for all Christians, we pray to the Lord. |
| All | Lord, hear our prayer. |

Reader    For all catechumens, and for the elect who are prepar-
          ing to enter the church this Easter: that this Lent will
          be a time of inspired preparation for them, we pray to
          the Lord.

All       Lord, hear our prayer.

Reader    For our parish and all the small groups: that all of us
          may grow as disciples, we pray to the Lord.

All       Lord, hear our prayer.

          *(Here the leader can invite members to offer any petitions
          or intentions they wish. Some quiet time should be allowed
          for this to happen.)*

Leader    Now let us join our prayers together in the prayer that
          Jesus taught us: Our Father... *(All pray the Lord's
          Prayer.)*

**4) Sharing Time**    There is probably too much material in a given Sunday's readings to cover everything in a 7:30 to 9:00 p.m. small-group
session. (And it is important to keep within the time limits set for the
small groups.) Although this will vary from group to group and from
meeting to meeting, you will probably have about 45 minutes for discussion. Therefore, we recommend that you focus on one or possibly
two of the readings (the gospel, obviously, has a certain preference).

The leader can begin with the appropriate question. Some samples
for each week of Lent can be found at the end of this chapter. The key
idea here is sharing, not judging. For example, when focusing on the
gospel, the leader may want to say something like this at the beginning
of the discussion period:

*"When we look at the gospel, we can raise two distinct but related ques-
tions: (1) what did the gospel writer mean at the time of composition; and (2)
what does the text mean now? This second step concerns us vitally. It asks:
What does the text mean to us today? While we must respect the original author, we also have to see the text in the context of our lives. Hence we can expect a variety of reactions. Thus, having heard the gospel, we should be big
enough to entertain different feelings. All of us can be enriched by sharing how
the gospel impacts our lives today. "*

Don't be afraid of silence after you ask the opening question. For the
leader, thirty seconds can seem like five minutes. Don't worry about it.
Discussion will come. Let someone else give the first answer and begin
the discussion. Don't always be the first to answer your own question.

If time is left after all the questions have been discussed, then ask: Does anyone have another insight to share? Again, don't worry about the silent time. One or another will have a reflection to share and, after others have shared, you may have a reflection of your own.

**5) Concluding the Meeting**  Be sure to conclude the meeting on time. It's OK to end a bit earlier than scheduled, but the meeting should not run overtime. People often make arrangements with baby sitters, relatives, or family members, and they need to know that they can leave at the predetermined closing time.

Make assignments for the next meeting as the last activity of the meeting. Seek volunteers for the next meeting to read the gospel or other passage, or to lead the prayer service.

A simple closing prayer is certainly in order. The leader might simply pray in his or her own words. For example, "Lord God, we thank you for the presence of your Holy Spirit among us this evening. Help us always to live and grow in the power of that Spirit." The leader could then ask others if they would care to add to the closing prayer with their own words, or ask the group to pray together a prayer that all of them know (the Our Father, Hail Mary, or Glory Be, for example).

# Sample Reflection, Prayer, and Questions for Small Group Use During Lent

*The following are offered as further samples for use in a small group meeting. The leader might begin by reading the reflection and leading the group in the prayer that follows. Each group of questions begins with a quotation. The first quote comes from the reflection of the week, the second from the first reading, the third from the responsorial psalm, the fourth from the second reading, and the fifth from the gospel. Again, it probably is not wise to attempt to cover all the readings or questions in one group meeting. Feel free to be selective, and to adapt any of this material to the needs of your group.*

## FOCUSING ON THE FIRST SUNDAY OF LENT

Genesis 9:8–15
Psalm 25:4–5, 6–9
1 Peter 3:18–22
Mark 1:12–15

**Reflection**

The biblical passages focus on accepting change. They imply that to live the gospel is to nurture the capacity for change. They suggest that the Christian life is not a static act of toleration but a willingness to respond to the needs of the moment. Gospel and change go hand in hand. Change is a difficult reality for most of us. We become set in our ways and happy with the *status quo*. We cannot imagine anything better or worse. Lent is, however, that unsettling part of the church year that welcomes and even demands change.

Our modern-day prophets rightly criticize the abuses in our midst. They point out the manipulation of human beings and the suffocation of the human spirit. They urge us to change ourselves by changing the system.

Our modern-day prophets also address our capacity to hope again. They challenge our unwillingness to imagine that things can be different and hence that there is light at the end of the tunnel. They call upon us to change by reaching out for God's grace.

**Prayer**

| | |
|---|---|
| Leader | Aware of our God's goodness, we offer these petitions to the Father through the Son: |
| | That we may recognize our need to change, |
| All | Lord, hear our prayer. |
| Leader | That we may discover hope in the midst of despair, |
| All | Lord, hear our prayer. |
| Leader | That we may be the agents of change for others, |
| All | Lord, hear our prayer. |
| Leader | That we may base our pattern of change on the life and death of Jesus, |
| All | Lord, hear our prayer. |
| Leader | Generous and loving God, give us the capacity to see that Good Friday moves on to Easter Sunday. Enable us to perceive that the empty tomb is the powerful reminder that everything is possible. We ask this through Christ our Lord. |
| All | Amen. |

## Questions for Group Use

*"Change is a difficult reality for most of us."*
Is this statement true in your life? Why do you think change is so hard? Has there been a time when you accepted change?

*"I set my bow in the clouds to serve as a sign." (Genesis 9:13)*
Is there a particular sign or symbol that reminds you of your ties with God? Why is it meaningful for you? In what ways does it call you to change?

*"Remember that your compassion, O Lord, and your kindness are from of old." (Psalm 25:6)*
The author of Psalm 25 sees pain as a faith opportunity. Based on your own experience, does this make sense? Have there been times of pain in your life when God seemed especially near and compassionate? In what ways?

*"Jesus was brought to life in the spirit." (1 Peter 3:18)*
Peter seems to suggest that an experience of "life" is always preceded by an experience of "dying." What do you think this means in terms of daily living? What forms of daily "dying" are you called upon to do? How are these opportunities for "new life"?

*"Repent and believe in the gospel." (Mark 1:15)*
Mark tells the story of Jesus' temptation in the desert. Though Jesus was tempted, he resisted. What is your usual reaction to temptation? Are there ways you can help yourself and others to make unselfish choices? What are they? What might you do today to begin the process of change for the better?

## FOCUSING ON THE SECOND SUNDAY OF LENT

Genesis 22:1–2, 9, 10–13, 15–18
Psalm 116:10,15,16–17, 18–19
Romans 8:31–34
Mark 9:2–10

### Reflection
The biblical passages concentrate on balancing relationships. They sug-

gest that to live the gospel is to develop and enhance our relationships. These relationships deal with the individual believer and God, the individual believer and the community of believers, and the individual believer and spouse, family, relatives, friends, and even enemies.

Relationships constitute the very fiber of life. By birth, marriage, baptism, etc., we acquire a variety of them. In order to lead a healthy, faith-filled life, we have to balance our relationships by setting up priorities and attending to their interconnection. Lent is a most apt time for looking into the connection between our relationships and our faith.

As believers, we clearly enter into a very special relationship with God. Baptism makes us daughters and sons of God. As such, we are on very intimate terms with Father, Son, and Holy Spirit. We are heirs to an unfathomable legacy.

As believers, we also enter into a very special relationship with the community of believers, the church. We are called upon to worship and pray as a community. The problem many of us face is the overcoming of a purely one-on-one relationship with God. In order to love, praise, and please God, we must love, praise, and please the community of believers. We must balance love of God with love of the community.

As family members and members of society, we also enter into very special relationships with spouse, family, other relatives, friends, and even enemies. Our task is not to isolate these relationships from our relationships with God and church. Instead, through our efforts and grace we are to forge a link that will unite all these relationships into a harmonious pattern. We have to balance them.

### Prayer

| Leader | Realizing our God's generosity, we offer these petitions to the Father through the Son: |
|---|---|
| | That we may deepen our relationship with the Trinity, |
| All | Lord, hear our prayer. |
| Leader | That we may be more aware of our bond with all believers, |
| All | Lord, hear our prayer. |
| Leader | That we may see our family and friend relationships within the context of love of God and neighbor, |

| All | Lord, hear our prayer. |
|---|---|
| Leader | That we may perceive that the art of living and believing consists in balancing our relationships, |
| All | Lord, hear our prayer. |
| Leader | Ever faithful God, grant us the wisdom to see our life with you as bound up with the lives of our sisters and brothers. Enable us to see that all relationships must ultimately end in you. We ask this through Christ our Lord. |
| All | Amen. |

## Questions for Group Use

*"Lent is an excellent time to examine our relationships."*
When you think about relationships in your life, where does God fit in? In what ways do you think your relationship (or lack of it) with God affects your other relationships? Are there ways you can grow in your understanding and appreciation of God's presence in your life? What are they specifically?

*"God put Abraham to the test." (Genesis 22:1)*
Abraham certainly understood this. How could he father a great nation if he sacrificed his son? Are there obstacles (problems, concerns) in your life right now that don't make sense? How are you dealing with this? Are there specific ways you nonetheless express your trust in God?

*"I am your servant; you have loosed my bonds." (Psalm 116:16)*
The psalmist has learned to praise God even in the midst of difficulties. By clinging to God, the psalmist was able to see his traumatic situation remedied. Are you able to praise God this way? Do you tend to blame God for difficulties? Why is this?

*"If God is for us, who can be against us?" (Romans 8:31)*
What does this mean to you, based on your real-life experiences? Do you believe that God is always with you, always concerned for you? Why or why not? What obstacles keep you from this kind of faith?

*"This is my beloved son. Listen to him." (Mark 9:7)*
In what ways do you listen to Jesus? In what ways is he speaking to

you now at this particular time in your life? How can you grow in your relationship with Jesus? Are there others with whom you have relationships who will support you in this?

## FOCUSING ON THE THIRD SUNDAY OF LENT

Exodus 20:1–17
Psalm 19:8,9,10,11
1 Corinthians 1:22–25
John 2:13–25

### Reflection

The biblical passages focus on doing God's will. They imply that to live the gospel is to live in accordance with God's plan. They also presuppose that believers can opt to live according to their own personal preferences. Hence tensions will arise when there is a conflict between God's will and our own. Lent serves as a special time for clarifying the driving force in our lives.

Autonomy and independence are values that we cherish immensely. We enjoy standing on our own two feet and making our own way in this world. In this scenario to be human is to be autonomous and independent. But laws—both God's law and human law—seem calculated to impede our drive toward full self-determination. Is it possible to be truly autonomous and independent and still carry out the will of God and others?

Once we get to the point where we accept the reasonableness of God's will and human laws, we then have difficulty with the very impersonalism of legislation. Somehow we have been trained to think that inhuman, impersonal forces stand behind God's will and other laws. What we need to do, therefore, is to make the effort to discover God and fellow humans behind all legislation.

We have been taught to be free *from*—free from unjust seizure, free from the IRS once we pay our taxes, etc. Unfortunately we have not always been taught to be free *for* —for our God, for our community, for our friends, even for our enemies. To do God's will is basically to exercise the obligation to be free for God and others.

All too often we attempt to do God's will and obey human laws because we feel we must. Our problem seems to consist in this—we do not search for the values behind God's will and human legislation. To that extent we have ceased to be human. To live the gospel is, implicitly at least, to recognize the values in God's will and human laws.

## Prayer

Leader    Aware of our God's concern for us, we offer these pe-
          titions to the Father through the Son:

          That we may see God's will more as a gift and less as
          a burden,

All       Lord, hear our prayer.

Leader    That we may link God's will with the person of our
          God,

All       Lord, hear our prayer.

Leader    That we may perceive freedom as also freedom *for*,
          not simply freedom *from*,

All       Lord, hear our prayer.

Leader    That we may search for the values inherent in God's
          will,

All       Lord, hear our prayer.

Leader    Ever loving God, grant us the wisdom to see your will
          as an expression of your concern for us. Enable us to
          find your presence in that will. We ask this through
          Christ our Lord.

All       Amen.


## Questions for Group Use

*"Independence is a value we cherish immensely."*
Is "independence" a value in your life? Why or why not? What does it
mean to you? How can you be free or independent when you have re-
sponsibilities? Can you really be free if you do God's will? How?

*"I, the Lord, am your God, who brought you out of...slavery." (Exodus
20:2)*
The text in Exodus suggests that our attachment to God actually "frees"
us. Does this ring true in your own life? In what ways are you a "slave"
to things? Where might you look for support in your efforts to be free
of things that enslave you?

*"The law of the Lord is perfect, refreshing the soul." (Psalm 19:8)*
The psalmist seems to have discovered a connection between God's

will and personal contentment. Have you had experiences of similar contentment? What were they? What do you think the psalmist meant by God's will or God's law? What does "God's will" mean to you personally?

*"Jews demand signs and Greeks look for wisdom..." (1 Corinthians 1:22)*
Paul told the Corinthians that the cross of Jesus was a stumbling block for some and "nonsense" for others. What does the cross mean to you? In what ways does it make Christianity different or more difficult for you personally?

*"Zeal for your house will consume me." (John 2:17)*
The scene of Jesus in the temple convinces us that Jesus put God's will before all other considerations. He took a stand that was very unpopular. Is there something right now about which you feel called to "take a stand?" What is it? What signs do you see that suggest that this might be God's will for you? How are you expected to know what God is asking of you?

## FOCUSING ON THE FOURTH SUNDAY OF LENT

2 Chronicles 36:14–17, 19–23
Psalm 137:1–2, 3, 4–5, 6
Ephesians 2:4–10
John 3:14–21

**Reflection**
The biblical passages address the issue of receiving new life. They suggest that to live the gospel is precisely that—to live a new life. They convey the powerful message that our God is not simply a God of endings but also of new beginnings. The God who bids us to live the gospel is the God who enables us to move beyond the realm of death into the world of new life.

We all seem to be lovers of spring. After the drabness and infertility of winter we yearn for the return of new vegetation. Our longing is not unlike that contained in the Song of Songs. "For see, the winter is past, the rains are over and gone. The flowers appear on the earth, the time of pruning the vines has come, and the song of the dove is heard in our land" (Song of Songs 2:11–12).

While we can anticipate new life in the world of nature, we find it more challenging to anticipate new life in the world of humans. The lingering illness of a loved one, the death of a spouse or child, the loss of a job, the erosion of friendship—life is full of experiences that appear to terminate our hopes and dreams. Sometimes we cannot even begin to imagine that somehow there is light at the end of the tunnel.

Our own sinfulness may be a glaring example of being mired in chaos with no expectation of the return of cosmos. We confront the painful reality of our own weakness. We can calculate the number of times we have fallen despite the best of intentions. In such situations our God is a distant, seemingly unconcerned being who only confirms the reality of our wretched state.

While Lent ushers in traditional practices of mortification (literally: putting to death), Lent also relentlessly presses on to the new life of Easter. Good Friday is not God's final word. The Easter Vigil brings the lushness of bountiful new life. To live the gospel is to be enabled to receive new life.

## Prayer

Leader  Aware of our God's involvement and concern, we direct these petitions to the Father through the Son:

That we may be empowered to accept new beginnings,

All  Lord, hear our prayer.

Leader  That we may learn to anticipate new life in the midst of the most trying situations,

All  Lord, hear our prayer.

Leader  That we may view our own weakness as the occasion for new life,

All  Lord, hear our prayer.

Leader  That we may always recall that Good Fridays lead to Easter Sundays,

All  Lord, hear our prayer.

Leader  Generous and loving God, kindly heed the requests of your people who may find it hard to imagine new life. Regard us as your Son's sisters and brothers and so fill our emptiness with new life. We ask this through Christ our Lord.

All      Amen.


## Questions for Group Use

*"To live the gospels is to live a new life."*
What connection does the gospel have to your life right now? In what ways does it affect your decisions at work and at home, your relationships, your leisure time? In your opinion, what kind of "new life" would come from living the gospel?

*"God has charged me to build him a house in Jerusalem." (2 Chronicles 36:23)*
In the bleakest hour, God seems to have the capacity to grant new life. Do you really believe that God has such a capacity? Does it ring true in your own experience? In what ways? How has God been a "God of new beginnings" in your life or in the lives of those around you?

*"By the streams of Babylon we sat and wept." (Psalm 137:1)*
To receive new life can mean to complain to God. Do you ever dare to complain to God? Why or why not? The psalmist suggests that the Israelites complained to God because they knew God could take action. Do you believe that God "takes action" in your life? In what specific ways?

*"God...brought us to life with Christ." (Ephesians 2:5)*
God's gift of life to us in Christ is also returned to us as "grace." How do you define grace? What is it and how does it work? How is the reality of grace obvious in your own life?

*"God so loved the world that he gave his only son that whoever believes in him may not die but may have eternal life." (John 3:16)*
Entrance into the Kingdom of God, Jesus later tells Nicodemus, depends on the outpouring of the Spirit. What do you think this statement really means? In what ways have you felt the "outpouring" of the Spirit? What does this outpouring have to do with grace? What connection is there between this and the "new life" the gospel offers? Do you believe that "new life" is really possible for you? Why or why not?

# FOCUSING ON THE FIFTH SUNDAY OF LENT

Jeremiah 31:31–34
Psalm 51:3–4, 12–13, 14–15
Hebrews 5:7–9
John 12:20–33

**Reflection**

The biblical passages focus on handling gifts. They suggest that to live the gospel is to develop the manner of handling gifts. They imply that we must be willing to accept gifts because that is the very nature of our God. Thus God gives because God is a giver.

We humans enjoy being in charge. We love to control situations because that implies that we have examined all the possibilities and have directed the course of action. To be surprised, however, is not to be on top of the situation. To be surprised is to be forced to acknowledge that forces beyond our effective control have influenced our destiny. In such a case our autonomy and independence seem to be in jeopardy.

In our more candid moments we do readily admit that our weaknesses outweigh our assets. Our record of failure indicates that the best of intentions and considerable degrees of effort will not attain our goal. These sobering concessions may direct us to Another who not only understands our plight but is also willing and able to help. Such help comes in the form of gift. We do not bring our merit cases before this God. We are simply moved to accept what we cannot achieve by our action. Basically, we are challenged to handle gifts.

Once we have discarded our attempts at control and have recognized our weaknesses, we are in a condition to recognize that the giving of unmerited gifts is an awesome manifestation of love. At this time we look beyond the world of control and weakness to a world of lavish giving grounded in love. To handle the gift properly is to announce that Another loves us for the sake of loving us. This is not the world of "you scratch my back, I'll scratch yours" or "I owe you one." This is a world of "I have called you by name: You are mine" (Isaiah 43:1).

**Prayer**

Leader     Aware of our God's capacity to love, we offer these petitions to the Father through the Son:

That we may believe in a God of surprises,

| | |
|---|---|
| All | Lord, hear our prayer. |
| Leader | That we may look beyond our faults to a Giver of gifts, |
| All | Lord, hear our prayer. |
| Leader | That we may acknowledge that our God's giving is a manifestation of our God's loving, |
| All | Lord, hear our prayer. |
| Leader | That we may dismiss our efforts at total control so that we might be able to accept such gifts, |
| All | Lord, hear our prayer. |
| Leader | Generous and loving God, grant us the ability to begin to fathom your concern and involvement. Enable us to recognize you in the act of giving. We ask this through Christ our Lord. |

## Questions for Group Use

*"The giving of unmerited gifts is an awesome manifestation of love."*
Would you rather give a gift or receive one? Do you usually feel obligated when someone does something for you, for example, invites you to dinner? How do you feel about God's gifts? In what ways do you feel "obligated" to do something in return?

*"I will be their God and they shall be my people." (Jeremiah 31:33)*
When you read this statement, what image of God forms in your mind? Do you picture an Old Testament prophet? A voice speaking from heaven? A parent who loves you? Where does your image come from? What does it mean for you that God is willing to be "your God"?

*"Have mercy on me, O God, in your goodness." (Psalm 51:3)*
How do you define the word "mercy"? Does it make you feel sinful or does it make you feel free? Why? In what concrete ways do you feel in need of God's mercy?

*"He offered prayers and supplications with loud cries and tears." (Hebrews 5:7)*
This text seems to point to the weakness of Jesus. Could Jesus really have experienced pain and frustration? How do you explain this? Why would coping with pain and frustration be the mark of a Christian?

*"I will draw everyone to myself." (John 12:32)*
In what ways do you feel called to imitate the universal love of Jesus? Does such a call conflict with Catholicism? Why or why not? In your opinion, what would be the cost for loving (and doing for) others, no matter their race, creed, or color, sex, or circumstance?

## FOCUSING ON PASSION (PALM) SUNDAY

Isaiah 50:4–7
Psalm 22:8–9, 17–18, 19–20, 23–24
Philippians 2:6–11
Mark 14:1–15:47

**Reflection**
The biblical passages focus on making discoveries. They suggest that to live the gospel is to be willing to make discoveries in situations where we least expect to be surprised. They imply that the Christian life demands that we set aside our preconceived notions about our God and other people and seek the unexpected. Ultimately our God is a God of disguises.

We tend to judge by externals. It is the outside that initially appeals to our imagination and conditions how we will respond. To that extent the exterior sets up the parameters for judgment. If it is appealing, we accept. If it is displeasing, we reject. The alarming fact is that all too often we are not aware of our prejudices.

Social status=divine status. We may divorce ourselves from those who say that wealth and standing are indications of God's pleasure, but, unfortunately, in daily life we often subscribe to such a view. The outcome is an assumption that the less than beautiful people cannot be God's intimates. Those at the bottom of the economic ladder and those at the top of the same cannot, so we think, have allegiance to the same God. The externals have once again preconditioned us.

Opposed to our prejudice is our God. Our God chooses to be manifested in an almost infinite variety of ways. Our God often prefers to be revealed in those who are social outcasts. The sorrowing, the ill, the down and out are but a few of the images of our God. To accept our God is to accept our God's images.

To live the gospel is to penetrate the external and discover the remarkable world of our God. This is a world that reverses our prejudices and overturns our presuppositions. To celebrate Lent is to make discoveries.

**Prayer**

Leader     Realizing our God's concern, we offer these petitions
           to the Father through the Son:

Leader     That we may overcome our tendency to judge people
           by externals,

All        Lord, hear our prayer.

Leader     That we may truly believe that social status and di-
           vine status do not necessarily go together,

All        Lord, hear our prayer.

Leader     That we may learn to discover our God in the most
           unexpected ways,

All        Lord, hear our prayer.

Leader     That we may truly appreciate our God as a God of
           disguises,

All        Lord, hear our prayer.

Leader     Generous and loving God, enable us to find your
           Son's image among all his sisters and brothers. Help
           us to be people who make discoveries. We ask this
           through Christ our Lord.

All        Amen


## Questions For Group Use

*"The gospel reverses our prejudices and overturns our presupposi-
tions."*
How do you form your judgments of others? Do your initial reactions
to people ever change? In what ways? Are there ways you can help
yourself and others to resist the temptation to judge by externals? What
are they?

*"I am not disgraced...I shall not be put to shame." (Isaiah 50:7)*
Recall a time when you had to endure intense suffering. Were you able
to see beyond that time? What helped you get through it? What did
you learn from this experience about yourself? About God?

*"O My God, I cry out by day, and you answer not." (Psalm 22:3)*
In the midst of difficulties, what is your attitude toward God? Do you

feel free, like the psalmist, to complain to God? Why or why not? Do you tend to blame God for your suffering? How do you express this?

### *"God greatly exalted him." (Philippians 2:9)*

Jesus stands before us as one who has endured suffering with hope and trust, and he has been exalted. Was it for "suffering" that Jesus was exalted? Why or why not? In your opinion, is suffering in and of itself a good thing? What purpose, if any, has it served in your life?

### *"Clearly this man was the Son of God." (Mark 15:39)*

To believe is to accept paradox and mystery, and to be open to new discoveries. Does this statement ring true in your life? In what concrete ways? If there are people you know who witness the kind of faith you would like to have, what is it that attracts you to them? What are some of the ways you have been "surprised" by God's gift of faith in your life?

## About the Author

Dr. John Craghan is associate professor of religious studies at St. Norbert College in De Pere, Wisconsin, associate editor for *Biblical Theology Bulletin* and has written for *The Bible Today, Emmanuel, Today's Parish, The Gathering Place,* and many other magazines. His recent books include *Yesterday's Word Today; Love and Thunder: A Spirituality of the Old Testament,* and *Psalms: Prayers for the Ups, Downs, and In-Betweens of Life.*